T0209529

MARCHING ON IN SPITE OF

Peace is What the Struggle Brings

Dedorah S. Brown

WESTBOW
PRESS®
A DIVISION OF THOMAS NELSON
& ZONDERVAN

WestBow Press books may be ordered through booksellers or by contacting:

WestBow Press
A Division of Thomas Nelson & Zondervan
1663 Liberty Drive
Bloomington, IN 47403
www.westbowpress.com
844-714-3454

ISBN: 978-1-6642-6127-3 (sc)
ISBN: 978-1-6642-6128-0 (hc)
ISBN: 978-1-6642-6126-6 (e)

Library of Congress Control Number: 2022905099

Print information available on the last page.

WestBow Press rev. date: 05/13/2022

Dedicated to Grandma Feenie, John Calvin,
Lil Royal, Shawn Anthony, and G-Bird.

Acknowledgments

Those marching on in spite of:
Grief and Trauma
Medical Matters
Addictions
Family Separation
Incarceration
Racism and Discrimination
Unfortunate Church Experiences
Abuse of any kind
Natural Disasters
Homeless Conditions
Education, Employment and Healthcare Disparities
Financial Hardships
Crime and Violence
Other Uncomfortable Truths

I appreciate these messengers of peace through being of service to others: JeNean S. Sanders, Jenell S. Wilson (and family), Damar K. Jones (and family), Marcella T. Lucas, Arlene Brown-Davis, Craig R. Elzy, Sonja M. Johnson-Calice, Patrice Williby, Dr. LaTasha M. Atkins, Michelle Bidwell, Shelly Gomez, Valencia Richard (and family), Barbara T. Cook, Kristi Broussard, My In-Laws, My Magnolia Family, Three the Phone Way and My Military Veteran Sisters and Brothers.

I also appreciate these individuals for sharing the message of peace through the use of music and song: Dante M. Bidwell, Destini Jenay L. Alston, Sherida M. Johnson, Emanee M. Drake, Emyri D. Drake, Emon M. Drake and Treyvon J. Horton.

Introduction

My peace was disturbed many times long before I was old enough to know what peace was. Then later in life, when I had somewhat of an introduction to what peace was, I erroneously believed that it was something that only others around me could have based on my presence and at times participation. Allow me to share a few as I explain how my views were formed.

When I was a little girl, my mother and I lived with my grandparents. It was a double-sided house, and my mother and I lived on the other side. There was a doorway in the living room that was always open to allow passage from one side of the house to other. That made it convenient for my grandmother to check on me while babysitting when my mother worked. It also made it easy for anyone visiting my grandparent's side to come over to my side of the house when she was out running errands, and I did not like that.

I tried to speak with my grandmother about it, but each time that I tried, the subject was changed. I told my mother that sometimes I did not like living there and I hated when she went to work. She explained why we had to live there and why she had to work, so the conversation ended there. That is when I began to pray. I prayed for myself, and I prayed that no other children in the world were afraid when their mothers went to work. I also prayed that God would let my grandmother realize what was going on.

Then the day finally came. My grandmother became aware. I was so happy! This is what I had been waiting and praying for! I would not have to be sad anymore. But oh, was I wrong. I was scolded. I was confused. I remember thinking, *No God. It was not supposed to go this way. I was not the one being bad. Tell her, Lord. Tell her!*

Eventually the yelling, cussing, and vulgar name-calling stopped and I was sent to bed. I cried and cried for what felt like hours. Then I heard my grandmother yell, "Stop all of that crying before I come over there and give you something to cry for!" I definitely did not want her to come over, so I managed to cry as quietly as I could. As I lay in bed thinking about how I was treated by my grandmother, I became angry and wanted her to get in trouble and yelled at by my mother.

Before my mother came home, my aunt and uncle stopped by the house. My uncle greeted my grandmother and came next door to my room to see me, and when he found me crying in bed, he began gently stroking the side of my face with the back of his fingers. Then my aunt came to the room. He asked her what happened, and she told him that they could talk about it in the car. Then they left. Something happened to me when they closed the front door behind them as they left. I knew that my aunt was told about what happened, but I thought that when she came to the room she would say something to me to make me feel better. But she did not even say hello.

Then it finally happened. Mama was home and everybody next door was gonna get it! I became happy, excited, and rescued. *Come on. Let's see who is going to get yelled at now! Come on!* I listened and listened but did not hear a word. I thought about getting out of bed to get to a spot where I could hear everybody getting in trouble, but I could not hear anything.

Finally, I heard my mother go into her bedroom and put down her things. She came to my room and in a soft voice asked me if I had to use the bathroom. I nodded yes. I got out of bed and went to the bathroom.

When I came out, my mother was standing there. I walked to her and stood directly in front of her. I had on a Disney-themed nightgown and no shoes. I remember that because I was looking down at my toes the whole time and at the way my gown was moving as I still trembled because of everything that had happened earlier that day. My mother asked me if I was hungry, and I shook my head no. Next she asked if I was thirsty, and again I shook my head no. Then she said something that I would never forget. She said, "OK then, go back to bed." The tremble went away. I could not feel a thing. The tremble was gone. I was physically able to see, hear, move, and function on the outside, but on the inside, I was light as a cloud and soft as cotton candy. It seemed as if there was nothing inside of my body. I walked to my room, got in bed, and do not know if I blinked my eyes again that day. Seems like there was nothing left of me.

During this stage of development, I thought that it may have been better for me if I no longer existed. Based on my despair and lack of maturity at that time, I did not realize that if my existence came to an end, it would have also ended all the beautiful things that I experienced after that. This includes the beautiful things that I currently have in my life and all of the future blessings that God has for me.

Eventually, I found peace with my grandmother for addressing the situation the way that she did. I found peace with my aunt's ability to see me in distress yet walk away without even saying hello. I found peace with my mother for not caressing me, for not kissing me, and for not sitting with me to talk to me about what I encountered. I truly believe that she responded according to the tools that she had. Then I found peace with my God for witnessing it all and allowing it to be. That was a difficult, life-altering experience. My three special ladies are in their heavenly mansions now, and I love and miss them dearly. Years and years before they left, although nonverbal, they made sure to let me know that they were sorry for their behaviors and that they loved me. I treasure my memories of them.

There are many stories that I can share with you about my struggles, including how I marched on in spite of and eventually found peace. But it is more important that you get to the part of this literature that is intended to encourage you to march on in spite of. Peace is what you deserve, and peace is what the struggle brings.

Marching Order Notes

I

You will find the courage to heal.
Keep looking within yourself.

Marching Order Notes

2

It is OK to cry.

Marching Order Notes

3

There is a silent part of your soul
that wants to be released.

Marching Order Notes

4

Change that hurtful recording that continuously plays in your head.

Marching Order Notes

5

Reconstruct your life. You will feel a whole lot better.

Marching Order Notes

6

Be assured that you will be whole again.

Marching Order Notes

7

Simplify. Get rid of the things and people who mean you no good.

Marching Order Notes

8

Keep your sanity instead of keeping the painful clutter in your heart.

Marching Order Notes

9

Acknowledge where the pain is coming from, and start there.

Marching Order Notes

10

To my survivors who were touched inappropriately, it was not your fault.

Marching Order Notes

II

Allow yourself to breathe, live, and grow. Rescue yourself from yourself.

Marching Order Notes

12

You are destined to heal. Just hang in there.

Marching Order Notes

13

Change is a process. Give it some time.

Marching Order Notes

14

Your strength and decision to heal are truly commendable.

Marching Order Notes

15

Your sadness of yesterday should not overshadow your hope for tomorrow.

Marching Order Notes

16

Persuade yourself that you matter, because you do.

Marching Order Notes

17

There is help for survivors like us.
Go get the help that you need.

Marching Order Notes

18

Someone can be delivered through your compassion to share your story as well as your journey to make it through.

Marching Order Notes

19

*If you want victory, take
your morals with you.*

Marching Order Notes

20

Do not just stare at your obstacles. Bring them down.

Marching Order Notes

21

Your life will put some demands on you that your challenges couldn't care less about. Choose the demands of your life, and leave your challenges by the wayside.

Marching Order Notes

22

Use both hands when reaching for happiness.

Marching Order Notes

23

Finding contentment with doing nothing can cause discontentment with your lack of peace.

Marching Order Notes

24

Keep striving for joy and peace, unless you are satisfied with unrest.

Marching Order Notes

25

*Get rid of the placebo version of yourself,
and let the real you take its place.*

Marching Order Notes

26

Although uncomfortable, we must face pressures and harsh circumstances that life may offer in order to get to all of the wonderful things waiting for us.

Marching Order Notes

27

You are well armored to win your battles.

Marching Order Notes

28

Educate yourself on the things that you need to know for personal growth.

Marching Order Notes

29

Spend time in environments and with people that are in harmony with your growth.

Marching Order Notes

30

Presenting in public as self-assured is one thing, but do you present that way when you are alone?

Marching Order Notes

31

Do not apologize for refusing to give power to those who mean you harm.

Marching Order Notes

32

Enjoy the luxury of being you.

Marching Order Notes

33

Do not let what you do not know trick you out of what you do know.

Marching Order Notes

34

You may not have your way with some of the things that you want, but that does not mean that you will not have your way with some of the things that you want.

Marching Order Notes

35

If you keep settling for less, that is what you will continue to have: less.

Marching Order Notes

36

There may have been many reasons why you fell short and did not accomplish what you hoped for. Shortcomings are inevitable at times, but giving up should never be an option. Go for what you want.

Marching Order Notes

37

Get excited about your life and how special you are.

Marching Order Notes

38

Changes can be hard to adapt to,
but in time, things will level off.

Marching Order Notes

39

Never lower your self-worth based on your depressive state, nor should you buy into a negative comment that some miserable person says about you. You know better!

Marching Order Notes

40

*If you set goals and do not reach them,
reset them and keep it moving.*

Marching Order Notes

41

You may feel one way now and later feel totally different, so do not let grief misguide you.

Marching Order Notes

42

Pay more attention to that motivational voice inside of you.

Marching Order Notes

43

Focus on the positive things around you because those things can lead you away from the negative things you may have stored in your heart and mind.

Marching Order Notes

44

Do not be afraid of the changes that you desire. Be afraid to stay in that unhealthy environment and state of mind where no peace resides.

Marching Order Notes

45

Get used to having peace.

Marching Order Notes

46

Live in a way that if today were your last day, you would be content with how you conducted yourself.

Marching Order Notes

47

Discard all grudges.

Marching Order Notes

48

Do something nice for someone who will never know your name.

Marching Order Notes

49

There is someone waiting to see the revitalized you, and that someone is you.

Marching Order Notes

50

Imagine a joyous future for yourself. Spend a little time with your thoughts. Now snap out of it, make a plan, and make it a reality.

Marching Order Notes

51

As bad off as you think you are, you can always be a good example for someone.

Marching Order Notes

52

Apologies may not be offered where the cruelty was generated, but you can still go and grow.

Marching Order Notes

53

There may be some things that come along intended to disempower you, but flip the script and disempower those things.

Marching Order Notes

54

Some days it is just hard to control your feelings, but as long as you control your response, you will be just fine.

Marching Order Notes

55

Power and healing are yours to have.

Marching Order Notes

56

The mistreatment that you experienced by friends, family, and foes can be used as a reminder that it does not matter where the misdeed came from. You can grow beyond it.

Marching Order Notes

57

Stop talking about what you can do, and do what you can do.

Marching Order Notes

58

The things that you are going through are grooming you for something better. Please believe that.

Marching Order Notes

59

You do not have to attack others. Attack those things that cause you discomfort.

Marching Order Notes

60

If negative memories are keeping you tied down, plan your escape route.

Marching Order Notes

61

You can have concerns about things without allowing them to overwhelm you.

Marching Order Notes

62

Your past prepared you for this day, so you are good.

Marching Order Notes

63

*Commit to your strengths and
not your weaknesses.*

Marching Order Notes

64

The more frustrated you are about your circumstance, the more effort you should put into changing it.

Marching Order Notes

65

You do not have to endure hardships just to be around those you care about.

Marching Order Notes

66

Many advantages can come from many of our adversities, so do not sweat it.

Marching Order Notes

67

In time something inside of you will tell you when and how to accomplish what you want.

Marching Order Notes

68

You will not always feel up to speed, but have compassion for yourself. You will go through some things that warrant you to take a break from time to time.

Marching Order Notes

69

Know the truth about who you really are. Just because someone tries to make you feel low and empty does not mean that you are low and empty.

Marching Order Notes

70

Do what you can with what you have as you wait for more to come.

Marching Order Notes

71

Work hard to put your problems behind you, and then work just as hard to keep them there.

Marching Order Notes

72

If you stop and think about it, many times when people fail you, it gives you the boost that you need.

Marching Order Notes

73

A person can be around you often and still not have the right intentions for being there.

Marching Order Notes

74

Sometimes you are better off where you are than where you want to be.

Marching Order Notes

75

Is it worse to be treated poorly by others or when you treat yourself poorly?

Marching Order Notes

76

Look at the issues that you have stashed behind your issues.

Marching Order Notes

77

If you want to live a better life, then live better.

Marching Order Notes

78

Spend less time trying to figure out the evil deeds of others and more time figuring out your future.

Marching Order Notes

79

You may have been through a lot that decreased your peace, but you made it through and you are still making it through.

Marching Order Notes

80

You can collect things that will keep you trapped, or you can collect things that can put you on higher grounds.

Marching Order Notes

81

At times you may be hurt by things, but please do not let those things destroy you.

Marching Order Notes

82

Love yourself, flaws and all.

Marching Order Notes

83

Get a better grasp on what you allow to hurt and offend you.

Marching Order Notes

84

March on in spite of what you go through because peace is what the struggle brings.

You and I are both aware that things can happen in our lives that may disrupt our peace. We are also aware that in our efforts to recuperate from those disruptions, it sometimes seems as if our emotions are sinking us to a lower state of mind. But we cannot surrender to the struggle. Instead, we must lean in and defeat those things intended to destroy our peace and potential. I know at times it can be hard, but again I encourage you to march on in spite of, because peace is what the struggle brings.

||| ||| | || ||||| | |||| ||| |||||| | ||||||| ||| ||| |||

Printed in the United States
by Baker & Taylor Publisher Services